The Myth of the Simple Machines

Also by Laurel Snyder:

Daphne & Jim: a choose-your-own-adventure biography in verse (Burnside Review Press, 2005)

Half/Life: Jew-ish Tales from Interfaith Homes, Editor (Soft Skull Press, 2006)

Up and Down the Scratchy Mountains OR The Search for a Suitable Princess (Random House Books for Young Readers, 2008)

Inside the Slidy Diner (Tricycle Press, 2008)

Any Which Wall (Random House Books for Young Readers, 2009)

The Myth of the Simple Machines

Laurel Snyder

No Tell Books 2007
Reston VA

Copyright © 2007 by Laurel Snyder

Published by No Tell Books, LLC

notellbooks.org

All rights reserved

ISBN: 978-0-6151-6132-7

Cover Illustration: Jaime Zollars

Cover Design: Maureen Thorson

Proofreader: Joseph Massey

Contents

The Machines

The Field Has a Girl- 9
The Simple Machines-   11
The Girl Learns Forfeit-   13
Paper Dolls-   16
Well: the Girl Who Falls-   17
Then Up— Shaken Morning-   19
Organizing the Stairs-   20
What the Dock Saw-   21
The Answer to the Puzzle-   23
Gravity of Halfway-   24
Happily Ever After-   25

Their Casings

Posture Matters-   29
Glass-   31
The Truth-   33
Good Morning-   35
I Covet Everything I Own-   37
Just There-   39
The Beast in the Cornfield-   40
New York Poem-   42
Technology-   43

In Technology

The Follies-   47
Weak Little Creatures-   48
Elegy for the Fair-   50
Sturdy Little Places-   52

In the Kitchen -   55
Logos- 57
Triptych of Useful Rules (Pictures)-   59
Triptych of Useful Rules (Words)-   60
Triptych of Useful Rules (Conclusions)-   61

At Rest

Half-sleep Segue-   65
Night 1 (The Wave)-   67
Night 2 (The Jade Plant)-   69
Night 3 (The Tide Pool)-   71
Night 4 (The Train)-   73
Night 5 (The Bake Sale)-   75

Acknowledgments-   79
About the Author-   81

The Machines

The Field Has a Girl

The sky has a blackbird.
The field has a girl.
The sky is to the field as
the field is to the sky, only

backwards. White is
to the blackbird as fear
is to the girl, despite
she's small and alone.

The bird has a wing
in the wind, a face in
the sky, and a shadow
on the girl.

There's a boy in
the field, too, and
the girl says she'd
like to hold the blackbird.

But, "Free isn't the same as
clean" says the boy, "or safe,
and anyway, the blackbird
doesn't want to be held."

The bird beats its wings.
The girl waits.
The sky creaks.
The girl says "I live in

this world," and means
it, but still she is small
in the field and beneath
the sky and the path of

the blackbird. "I live
in this," says the girl.
"Alone," says the girl.
Things become quieter.

Things become.
"No matter what you
may do with your life,"
says the girl.

The Simple Machines

Here—a lever as helpful as a hand
and a pulley that whimpers from the ceiling,
but in this small room
they aren't connected by the right problem.

Here—a door to outside, but the girl
doesn't face it, so you be the girl.
In this small room, your thin red sweater, your too short skirt,
be always tugging at a crooked hem.

The room will get cold and your legs might turn pale,
but if they shiver, face a helpful corner,
and when holding both hands clenched before you,
try to have something in them.

"Choose," you'll say to the corner, unfolding both hands.
In each you'll find fire that leaps,
then devours like a person, but beautifully.
You'll be afraid.

So you'll turn to your words,
to your simplest solutions.
You'll open your mouth to say,
but what will come out? Laughter.

You'll close your eyes, wave your arms
a little, but you'll only find laughter.
In the tight hot room, your laugh won't loosen
anything, not even the lid of a jar.

When the room echoes
and spits the laugh back,
all the glass in each window
will jump to the yard.

The Girl Learns Forfeit

1
The girl's sure
that the silt
in her tea
is ground glass,

and she thinks
she'll die soon.

She wants to tell
the boy, but they're
playing chess,
and it's his turn,

so she gropes
at her belly instead.

The girl's sure
she's bleeding
on the inside.
She lets go

her teacup, but the cup
lands upright

on the table,
so everything's
fine, and it's easy
to keep going.

2
The girl's considered
slitting her throat,
but she's afraid
of intention.

She wants an accident,
but she's never had one.

Somehow, the girl
just never walks when
it's time to stand still, and
so walking can't kill her.

Like the magic
of how she was born

breathing, a simpler
version of thought,
but with her breath
and some air.

She doesn't try.
She doesn't try.

She's sure things fall
from the sky
because it's the easiest
place to fall from.

3
The girl thinks:
even the sky
is falling heavily
from the sky,

though somehow she's
not beneath it when it falls.

Some people
call this luck,
but the girl
knows better.

She's a fish who can live
on a plate.

Now the girl
tosses the game
into the air, so the air
is falling around her,

raining little men
and men on horses,

who knock the teacup over.
So the game is ruined,
but never finished. "What else
could I do?" asks the girl.

Paper Dolls

This is the shape of some words,
but not just.

This resembles the story
of a girl, but not just.

This is called
making it daily.

Go ahead. Take scissors,
and with a snip, make a girl.

Might as well make many.
They'll all look alike,

but some will hold fewer hands
than others.

You'll see what I mean,
but not just.

Make a flurry
of paper bits that won't

seem to end, and what else
might you have made?

Well: the Girl Who Falls

1
The girl who falls
can't swim, displaces

the water. What we call weather
is sometimes like this,

around us, and with us
inside everything. Winter.

2
The girl falls,
and a cold place in the ground

displaces fear, but the girl
won't have it. She says to her fear,

"Hurry back with a rope
or some dinner. Hurry back

with your very strong arms."
She waits. Some birds come

to see her and some birds
come to see. She's lucky. Now

it's spring, so there are fireflies
and the hole doesn't seem so deep.

Her voice, loud in the hollow,
shakes the ground, shakes

a little. How loud it sounds
inside the earth.

Then Up— Shaken Morning

The girl took the steps at breakneck speed.
"What?" And the world went with her—
steps slanted, feet fell, braced for bottom.

Then up, shaken beside an azalea.

Some light took shape, leaked onto earth,
onto sight, leaked onto trees. The house stood, ate the air
behind the steps, stretched, took all the wood and a window.

"A girl could live in a place like this."

There was earth pushed right up to the first step, wrinkled
blades of soft grass and a few new bits of clover.
The girl (as if to cry) leveled head to hands, but then changed

her posture. She felt the moving of what should,

and smiled. "I never was here before this, but now—"
One girl. Sturdy house in a nameable season.
Steps with banister, sorely in need of fixing.

Organizing the Stairs

1
Where there are no hills,
there are no valleys,
but there are sometimes
stairs and landings.

The girl doesn't count
those stairs, only pays
attention to them.
Consequently, she's fine.

2
The hill that isn't—gets made
from no earth and no stone,
is frequently covered
by nothing green,

and the valley is no amount of air.
Can you imagine how much there is
to miss, picture an absence
greater than what went?

3
The girl won't count each thing before her.
This stair makes need for the next stair,
and so on. Stairs in their proper order
are stairs. Otherwise, other stairs.

"You have to assume something
if you want to get somewhere."
No matter how absent the world may be,
the girl knows how to arrive.

What the Dock Saw

1
The moon shone on the bottle, girl inside.
At rest, it was resting. It was still
where the girl slept, cheek to glass. Hushed.

She was done with the water, but first
the water had done with her—nearly
finished her with one clever wave.

And how the bottle escaped the wave
was a miracle of division. It was a strong bottle.
The girl was fine, if held. They were two vessels.

So if a gull, white rustling in darkness,
found himself less white in that darkness,
less lit from above—he could hardly blame

the moon its grudging love.
The gull cried hollow, outside the moment.
The girl slept on. The bottle was full.

The moon felt sad, but when he turned
to them, he turned on them. The girl turned
in her sleep, and the bottle shivered.

2
The girl crawled out, and into morning.
All pale and simple, she found: Herself,
with sand on scrambling knees; Water,

held by waterline, now inching an apology;
Bottle, empty object; Moon, gone.

Instead, the sun. A sure sun and almost
where she looked, almost everywhere.

The Answer to the Puzzle

The answer to the puzzle
is the mauled bird on the sidewalk,
and the feathers.

The answer to the puzzle
is that things keep getting less lovely,
but more interesting.

When the girl falls
through the air from the top
of a very tall building,

she sees everything
rush past her in great detail
but with little promise.

Onlookers see, "Some girl
cutting through the air
like a knife cuts through water."

They gasp and say, "How terrible.
That poor girl. It's just awful."
And it really is. A moment.

Gravity of Halfway

Then one tree fell slightly. Because gravity

was willful, but tired.
Sad, sad gravity of the tree halfway.

Any bird was nervous to land.
Snakes refused, thinly, easily,
to glide beneath.

Each sun, in thoughts of speckled light,
of finding color, left the tree
cold to glint and rifle some other.
Moss grew uneven, slantwise, sorry.

Each shadow too. And the girl
walked, when she walked,
two meadows over, to neglect
the uneasy tree. Patience, effort.
Her shoes got wet when she went.

Happily Ever After

The wolf bears down
on the girl, thin in the corner.
His teeth are as sharp

as the shoulder blades beneath them.
Everyone's hungry.

The wolf heaves and moans,
his ribs shift beneath his pelt.
He gnashes and drools,

chews (through) his words,
"Just where I want you."

She's small, a house
of straw, of twigs, of air.
She's a sheep in sheep's clothing.

She whispers sadly,
"Just where I want you."

It's always the girl, really.
In every doorway, behind each tree.
She's paddling down-river on a raft.

She's licking the batter from the spoon,
pumping your gas, "Thank you ma'am."

She's every wolf, every rib, every snarl.
No matter how she tells her story.
No matter what the frame looks like.

The curtains blow strangely.
The window's open wide.

But that doesn't mean
she went through it.
The wolf's full—this room is empty.

But where's our clever girl?
She's over there, behind that door.

Their Casings

Posture Matters

1
When my tea gets cold I like to cry,
and there's a run in my stockings
that won't ever end. It gets me.

But isn't it endearing?
Tell me I'm endearing.

In a straight-backed chair,
with my eyes closed, head back,
hair falling, limbs just so, I'm waiting for you.

Because posture matters,
and the smell of where I was—in my hair.

2
The day we climbed to the top
of the barn, there was a blizzard
and it was everywhere.

The white storm seemed
outside me, but it wasn't just.

Of course our cheeks were cold.
Of course my chin seemed to reach your shoulder.
I planned it that way.

The sky seemed worth stopping for
once I told you it was.

3
At the grocery store, I'm
"That quiet girl in the blue coat."
I shop alone.

I like myself against the Bartlett pears
and the smell of pears.

Do I look sad?
I think I'm very pretty, sad and alone
in the grocery store.

A man stands near me sometimes,
in the story with the pears and the blue coat.

Glass

It's not enough to be consistent.
I want things what they seem.

Glass is always liquid,
but the difference between shatter
and swim matters. Sometimes
I pass through a surface.

Like it or not, this is for you,
so pay attention.

I was born in Maryland,
where white dogwoods grew all over.
I thought they held the big damn
country together with their roots.

So what if nothing is true?
It used to feel like it was.

Maybe you've never been wrong,
but then I can't believe a word you say.
The things that don't work
are the important things to have wanted.

You should have all this
figured out by now.

None of the people I really love
are here, so you feel true.
None of the people who love me are here,
so I forget meals.

I could have told you when I was six
what wealth was—

too much, the things
you won't really need.
A house full of strangers,
all the lights on.

The Truth

Listen. My grandmother
died and we burned her

up in a fire but when we
went to dump her ashes,
in water—because water
is cool and makes us feel

better—she refused to be
put under. She floated

until my uncle held her down.
He forced her—to swallow the
end and the water to swallow
her body. Then we drove

away quick. Didn't stare
too long at the spot. She was

horrible, my grandmother,
and that's the truth, though
my uncle pretended. "She
was a good old girl, just

the dog done lost her bite."
But no. "But no she

never did," we told him.
If only she had. The witch.
There she was—rising, biting
at us from the very end.

Trying to claw her way to
beyond her welcome, which

died about the time she
began. It's a terrible thing—
hatred. Of family, the dead,
water that isn't heavy enough

to pull things down and keep them.
"I love you," I said to her as she died.

"Yes, but you love lots of people,"
she growled back faintly.
"Not enough," I should've told
her then, "nowhere near."

Good Morning

I didn't set the alarm, but then it went off.
Loud, and lucky me—so the dogs began

howling into the morning that wasn't yet.
The dogs are good at predictions.

Everything is a chain reaction. The dogs
wake up the birds, who wake up the coffeemaker.

Everyone has a job to do, so it was a day.
Yawn and shower as a siren passed. Some toast.

Only then the sun. Only then
there was a body in my body.

The dogs have been turning up everywhere
this year. Live in the hedges.

With their bellies and their legs. Peeking
hungry, from behind mailboxes, gimpy.

I love the dogs, but sometimes.
There are just so many of them.

Dog One and Dog Two can't get along.
Dog Three is sad, and Dog Four forgets

things more and more each day.
It's difficult for the rest of us. It is.

Dog Five left us and we worry.
And poor Six won't come close enough

to learn his name. We don't know why.
We don't know why. It has something

to do with routine, or maybe prediction.
He knows something, Six does.

It isn't good, but he needs it. His
alarm. I'll fill his bowl by the hedge.

I Covet Everything I Own

I envy the deeply green spider-plant—
how it drapes its spiky self
over the paler green arm of the sofa,
and the way the green drapes. My sofa.

My spider—it graces the velvet
with a thin finger, an offshoot of outside,
a crooked tendril. My tendril. How it washes
everything with green light—and I'm hungry.

Oh! The memories too. I covet every
gone year, every wet summer, every early supper
on a citronella porch. I envy Tennessee, kudzu
jealously vining the mountains, humidity—

that pillowed air folding like damp sheets
until starry dusk. I can't even smell it anymore,
can't quite. I covet drunk and tired and quietly,
you. I covet my own thighs last year.

It isn't the things I haven't had,
can't dream, quite recall. Or the things
I see in people's pictures. But
my own tightly wrapped hunger for

my own—my own—the things I've lost,
or forgotten, wrapped and folded, hidden,
and laid with care in an attic, a trunk
for someday's children. I covet the kids

I used to know I'd have, but don't
believe in anymore. It's all
in my belly or brain, all the rasping
things I was, wanted, can't contain.

Just There

There are some things
in the world. In it. Not about
it, or your head all cloudy.

There are some things
you just can't just slap
an old farmhouse onto.

Some things soup won't
wash away. Or a highway.
Some things are just there.

This is why I invented bed
and tomorrow and beer
battered onion rings.

Everything counts
sheep. Everything
fights a battle and loses.

You have to give up
at least once each day
to be a person.

If you don't close your
book you won't even—
you won't ever—

The Beast in the Cornfield

> *If I could fuck a mountain*
> *Lord, I would fuck a mountain*
> —Will Oldham

1
When I say I fucked a mountain,
I mean I made love on a hill.

I'm not as intense as all that,
but I was when I was sixteen and it was fast.

A train went by, took longer than we did,
so I left. Sixteen.

2
A real enemy is a rare gift.
A great white shark is a blessing.

We kill the wrong way,
with love and too much talking.

We hold back, apologize nicely, forgive.
I want something else. Sixteen!

3
But instead I have you. You staring
at that corn field, saying nothing. You sighing

at that huge green sea, with all its tides
like rulers. You tell me they run straight

until a wall happens. To them. Or something.
What's that supposed to mean?

4
You notice the stars too. You sigh, "Everyone
is hiding something, sweetheart. Even the night."

Are you kidding me? Nobody hides anything.
They only try. We are all windows. Easy.

Instinct tells sharks to swim forward,
but still—nature is no excuse.

Stop sighing. I hate you. We could have
been doing it this whole time.

New York Poem

This town—things
are either small by necessity
or loudly proclaiming their size.

Yesterday was something,
a honeydew moon I bought from a very small man on a corner.
There's a constellation, a map

of such things sold on corners, things not otherwise
connected. The map looks like a map.
We call it, "Our map."

My first day in town—a woman
said to me, "Darling—You have
such a lovely face. Have you thought

of modeling?" I laughed, slapped my ample.
"But no, they use larger girls now," she said.
"The health thing is big this year."

Square footage. Heels on women's shoes,
portions of shrimp and salad. Cars and trees
and longings, too. "What'll you have?"

To figure this out. This city,
woman, my constellation. All of it
mine now, ample and loud, full.

All of these things—screaming
for space or screaming with space. Shoved
into corners but flailing their arms.

Technology

Trying to grow a machine from inside this flower—

is like trying to grow a flower from inside this machine.
I don't believe in silver petals, in leaves unfolding like tender cogs.
I don't believe in hybrids, in the shiny cyborg bouquet.

I'm obsessed with this.

My dream therapist would say, "I'm totally fascinated
by your erratic behavior and your uncanny self-awareness.
I can't possibly fix you, but by all means, continue."

My name is Laurel and I'll be your waitress this evening—

When I get to the table with the big ugly menus, a fat woman
    is drinking
straight from the scratched water pitcher on the table, so I set
    down a glass
in front of her and I say, "Ma'am, why are you drinking from
    that water pitcher?

because we all have to drink from that, you know—"

Now it's time to go to bed. I'm wearing just my bra, so it's
    almost me.
You're reading a blue paperback, and when I stretch out beside
    you, peer down,
run my hand over my own breasts, cup my own belly, I say,

"Look at this senseless landscape from where I am. See?"

In Technology

The Follies

Never mind that there's a backdrop—

The truth's in a perfect flush of soft arms,
waves of ocean moon and blue night, pale and careful
foam and all the light flesh and soft grace

of yellow hair and the quick smiles of girls girls girls

stored in a theater. Violin tremors. The sound
of running water in a high hollow voice and then the swell
of some perfectly drunk band to fill in the outlines.

The thinner the magic, the sooner it tears—organza,

the dress comes off easy—chiffon, you can almost see
through anything if you peek. Is there a story here?
Or just beauty at large—and a few words we don't have

anymore. Pleurisy, consumption, the grippe.
Ruby, sable, Imogene, sealskin, speakeasy.
Alone, the parts just won't do. Enough.

Shine on, harvest moon.

Weak Little Creatures

1
Skin, a light cloth, easily pulled.
Pull=barely. Pull=mild.

We get dealt only what we will bear. Or death.

2
There are true things and also nice things,
but they aren't the same things.

Nice, that's *nice*. Not *good*.

3
A woman flutters, *Is today Tuesday? I lose track—
of everything.* A woman wants something to hold.

Babies make little sense, defy reason.

4
She wanted a baby, but then she didn't.
She wanted God, and besides—

Why else would you?

5
It might be awful. How could it not?
That weak baby, all hers—

Women make babies, and they can *die*.

6
Some things are true. Not nice, but true.
Eventual=true. And also God.

Or maybe a baby, who might—

7
Because oh, skin gasps, and rips open.
Terribly, as it's meant to.

Babies are tiny, and mean.

8
Women make babies, *so* they can die.
The women I mean, so *they* can die.

We can't explain it. Yet—

9
Women make babies because.
God hides under blankets.

We hope everything is true.

Elegy for the Fair

You used to be able.
To run away is to be lost.

Now, there is something.
Everywhere, in every corner.

Not dust, but thinking words.
Speaking with people.

And purpose in every unturned.
Freight car and hitchhike, dead.

Now, with the empty filled.
With classified ads in each pocket.

It is harder than *that*.
To flee, to fly, to lose.

Yourself in the circus.
Yourself in the fair of colors.

Each color has a name.
Each fortune-teller is a skeptic.

You are a skeptic, know *better*.
The fortune tellers are dying.

Because they have been wrong.
The clowns are unfunny.

Once, in a city, rain.
Out went the fair, lights.

And there in wet, in magic.
Was an old man who had a game.

Some balls and bottles and prizes.
Nobody wanted anymore.

The world was unimpressed and the rain.
Was going to keep on.

And the man was not a carnie.
Anymore the world is too smart.

Purpose means many things.
What we have lost has not always fled us.

Sturdy Little Places

1
There was a steady fire burning
beside the river last Tuesday.
Two men warmed their hands.
They had a fishing pole but no fish,
and they thought it was their river.

You can't claim one object with another.

2
Which of those two mountains
is taller? They look the same
from where you stand, but altogether
different from the stark place—
where real measurements get made.

The place you choose to stand in, won't change the way you stand.

3
It's only seasonal, this lingering
cough, no matter how long the season.
Here's some tea with lemon.
Here's a good red blanket.
A full night's sleep will mend.

If your floors slant, you'll either adjust or rebuild.

4
It's wrong to shoot the dog
for what the cat did.
It's wrong to hit hard.
It's wrong to remember

what someone else wants to forget.

And your great nation is built on arbitrary adjustments.

6
It's a bad idea to cry wolf
when you aren't the shepherd.
A house of cards is a weak house.
Pleasure is a full house, but strong.
There are many ways to build.

Take this hammer, love. It fits any hand.

7
The smell of burning leaves
won't warm cold fingers,
is the smell of something being lost,
is coming through the window
of your dusty truck.

Before you can determine the effectiveness of anything, you should understand
    its goal.

8
Love is a bear trap, or a shallow pit
covered with grasses of another color.
Love is a lever. A sturdy something
to hold. And/or love is a law, a great
nation, a mountain, a stone in the river.

Outside your truck—speed and wind, and the places you pass.

9
God is a fine electrician.
He'll replace every wire,
keeping his small hands dry.

He can loosen your grip on that
steering wheel any time you want.

Gravel on a rough road will never stop scrambling (for safety).

In the Kitchen

God clacks his spoon
against his bowl,
his bowl against his table,
and his table against
the white walls of his house.

God's impatient or just
keeping time.

The soup isn't hot enough yet,
so he waits, writes his name
on a yellowing cookbook
where the dust is thick and moist.
He writes *God*.

God's a sloppy housewife.
He sits on the counter,
stares at his slippers,
watches the pot of soup
until it boils on the stove.

It smells like cabbage and turns the day
into what God calls *supper*.

God reaches for the salt and thinks
about his dreams, how they're full
of other people, other things.
God tears into the bread and it feels
nice, close against his fingers.

He finds his teacup cracked
and whimpers. He can fix it
but it will still have been broken.
God pulls the teacup to his belly
and holds it there, hard.

He says to the room,
Look! Something might happen.

Logos

1
And this earth was once
confused and tangled
and darkness.

And God called to the light,
Day! And to the dark
he called, *Night!*

And suddenly, he saw giant
God-fingers making shapes
through the murk.

And God called
to the fingers and to
the things they felt.

And in the white room
a man watches his hands
beat and bruise a thing.

And he relents and breathes
into the white room, and sees
that the thing is now just that.

And so he calls to the thing
and the moment and the air
hovering in the room. *Thing!*

And then again he calls,
clearly and flatly: *Time of Death: 12:32.*
He calls to the time.

And elsewhere, *Our Father who art—*
You fucking whore you fucking slut—
I think We'll call you Emma—

And elsewhere, *I will—*
My body which will be given up for you—
My name is X and I'm an alcoholic—

    2
    Nobody can say *word*
    is not the nature
    of saying. What we are.

Triptych of Useful Rules (Pictures)

1
No darling, oceans don't
freeze. Now come away

from the water and we'll
get some nice lunch.

But the briny ocean will freeze, just as the kettle
will sing. Only not while we're watching.

She's waiting for us to turn our heads,
but she has her price, her point of bending.

2
Sometimes we catch the kettle.
Sometimes—icebergs.

3
The man you live with redefines intimacy
again and again, and you let him. You scribble

in your dictionary, crossing out
the extra words with a thick black pen.

Rules are not lies, but they're negotiable,
and made of something ordinary. Made of

chewing gum that re-softens in your mouth
each time you pull it from the bedpost.

Triptych of Useful Rules (Words)

Ocean-
1.) We went there one summer and a nasty seagull sneaked a slice of lunchmeat from my paper plate without ever landing. 2.) Always Atlantic, gray and colder than she looks.

Kettle-
1.) Old yellow thing with a burnt handle, stained, but still perfectly useful, for goodness sake. 2.) Always with its inch of tired water, but you can't see how tired it is, because the water is inside. 3.) Eventually, tea.

Intimacy-
1.) You'll know it when you see it. 2.) Anything that lasts longer than it needs to, sentence, look, hand on shoulder. 3.) I mean to say, it lingers. I mean both things.

Triptych of Useful Rules (Conclusions)

1
You're driving past an unfamiliar girl in an unfamiliar town when you turn the steering wheel, turn yourself the wrong way onto a one-way street. You can tell immediately that something's very misplaced, but it takes you a second to realize that the misplaced thing is you. It takes you even longer to find the words, *wrong direction*.

2
By then, the woman who was driving toward you in her blue sedan is already up on the grass in somebody's yard, screaming and shaking a fist. Your car's still moving, keeps moving. So you turn the steering wheel again, slam your foot on the gas, tear through an intersection, change lanes three times, weave, pull out of town. Now you're on a highway, on a two lane highway alone, singing with the radio, laughing out loud.

3
Direction-
1.) The way you're facing at this moment in time. 2.) The other way, the way you can't see yet. There behind you. Arbitrary, necessary, there.

At Rest

Half-sleep Segue

Bad days breed heavy nights,
strong desires.
Hunger works hard if you let him.

"Will work for food, or the promise of food."
"Will work beneath a kitchen window, unattended."
"Will steal warm pie from ledge."

On a Tuesday night, the girl dozes and dreams
of a fireplace. She's a whisper, a murmur in a slip,
dancing in a slip made of diamonds beside a fire.

The walls are close. The air is warm
red wine and there is candlelight, from somewhere
golden behind her. Deeply golden.

She's hushed in her heavy slip, dancing slowly
on a thick carpet, alone. When she bruises, she feels
like money, like extra money. She's a full pocket.

This is night. The dream is like water
so she needs it, but she wakes anyway
and the glaring ceiling won't let her sleep.

She feels a body breathing beside her
and shuts her eyes as quietly as ever she can.
She resolves to dream harder next time.

She feels the body shift, feels an arm
come round her coldly, heavily. Shh.
A cold other body is best when left

absolutely still, snoring and softly. Shh, don't wake it. "I'm that girl in the bed. I'm that sleeping ventriloquist."

Night 1 (The Wave)

I was a refugee in a warehouse, tapping on shoulders, but I didn't know why. Tapping on shoulders, circles of shoulders, I got tired. Nobody talked to me. There was a foot of water around my ankles and I pulled the ankles through the water, a cold wet answer. I found a window, trudged over to the window, low and long like the warehouse. I peered through the window and found an ocean, a friendly dog of an ocean.

Was I a little scared? Maybe, but then he came on all warm and disorganized, rushed to meet me in his sloppy way, nudged the wall below me and I trusted, leaned to touch him. I felt the ocean and he had not enough purpose to be cruel, not enough speed or method. He rushed against the wall happily and I climbed out into him, out into the dream.

The water was huge and purple, great and full, a warm soft landscape at my waist. I was in the landscape, a tree inside the landscape. Far off, the water was deeper, tall and above with waves. But the waves were old low mountains, curved and cleavaged and calm. They never crested or caught, and I couldn't seem to sink, not even when the undertow wanted me. I wanted him too.

One wave—he came for me, pulled me warm to the top of himself, him tall self, I slid up his side and he was the highest mountain, full and round and smooth, a pillow of water, a drowsy current. My skin felt easy and outside me, nice against the warm of the wave.

My eyes were open but I wasn't looking, didn't need to. I was up to the summit. I was the summit and then slowly down myself I slipped, to become the girl sliding gracefully down. There were people below, elsewhere and safe, I knew, but not where or how closely.

The lovely wave carried me and the world grew wet with the trailing of our hemline as we swept softly at our constant speed. We showed the world our petticoat. The wave was my full skirt in the warm sun, in the wet world where everything moved but nothing was lost or gained. Just warm, just warm and full, we carried ourselves around.

Night 2 (The Jade Plant)

In my hand—a red clay pot with a two inch mouth, so small I forgot it each time I looked away. The little pot was real, firm in my palm, secure with its sprig, its tiny wand of green. Dead center in black black earth, the stem's lonely leaf was so narrow, so thin. It was too small to be anything recognizable, too small to be anything.

The air hummed and I was a giant, I took my eyes from the leaf, from the little pot. I studied the walls, which were bare. I studied the hum.

When I looked back down, burdened by the leaf, he seemed larger, but I couldn't be sure. He was still so thin and nervous. I glanced away again and missed a moment of unfurling, a small leaf unfolding himself into existence. I played along, crooked my head over my own shoulder, examined the wall behind me.

He grew while I was away. He pulled his other hand from his pocket and then there were two leaves on the stem, both small but full and unfolding. He wanted

And I understood, gave him a minute. I studied the ceiling, counted to a certain number, lowered my eyes again. And Oh! He had grown, spread a tiny canopy, an array, an umbrella over his earth. I raised the jade plant to my eyes and peered into his world, found it moving, shuddering as though about to be.

Burst forth, burst into obvious life.

Now I looked away because I had to, because my wonder demanded that my eyes close briefly. But then the thick smooth leaves became the branches of a tree. The tree's edge spilled into my curled fingers and I could not look away. Things were moving. Deep under the canopy—a little house and the music of voices, of hammers beating and saws moving on timber. I heard a cry

And my eyes fought their way through the dense foliage to a tiny girl leaning against the tree, her arms circling the trunk. She sobbed and her tiny head shook. Her knees bent into tiny angles as she slid to the dark ground. I thought she would break.

She was pale, so perfect in her white dress beneath the shade of the tree. I spoke to her and my voice was giant, too clumsy to be heard. Then the tree changed.

It was ready, it turned red and I could smell an apple roasting, could see a thin line of smoke. The smoke rose and was lost in the big room. The smell came then of fall dying into chill, of mulch. When the leaves fell, they crushed everything, everything. They killed whatever was beneath them and then became only more dark earth.

The leaves spared one thin dry stem, which I plucked and swallowed. I swallowed the stem and scattered the world as best I could. It was beautiful.

Night 3 (The Tide Pool)

You and I, we were beside a deep tide pool. A rock cliff towered gray and cold above us, but the sun was rising over the water, so there was no shadow, no shade. The cliff was high and the beach was wide and our pool was deep, though all the other tide pools were shallow and warm. Ours was a bowl, a teacup of still cold water. We sat,

looked into the bowl, but first could only see the surface. Hard and tight and smooth, the line where air met water seemed flawless. Only then one slender creature, one insect like a stray hair, creased the smooth. I set my eyes to look in, shifted my eyes and saw beneath, and the insect melted away in a moment. Deep and down was the bottom, was the color of the floor, was a bed of flowers.

A bowl deep with anemones, thick blossoms. All the colors of chrysanthemums, golds and purples, bunched closely in a fist, leaving no room, no place to slide a finger between, no way to pluck. A deep bowl of petals, and we beside the bowl. Beside the teacup's steep rim. Me with my legs crossed beside me and you crouched like a cat, aimless and intent, hungry with no fish to follow, eyes darting.

I reached out an arm, couldn't help it, pointed a finger, and the water swallowed my hand. We were full of open mouths, full of sun on shoulders and wonder and silence. We reached my finger down to grace a petal and the garden shivered. The petal was soft and she folded or withdrew or died.

We carved a path with our faintest touch, drew a light line with the back of my hand. I waved. The touch was almost something else, so faint as to resemble another sense. The back of my hand saw the flowers, my skin heard each petal, smelled each distinct moment of folding inward. But no pressure, no weight. We carved lightly, accidentally, and the color of the path we made was darker somehow, like velvet pushed the other way.

Then there was a man above us, naked in the sun, a landscape of bones and dark hair. So little like our bowl of color, our bed of water, our faint touch. His body was a voice, a rude noise, so much a naked man.

The man tried to kneel beside the bowl, but changed his mind. He paused, straightened and then walked down the beach, his arms crossed over his chest as though to contain something.

The bowl was still there but the day was changing. The insect was back, the sun was behind a cloud and the flowers were very far away. When we wondered where the man had gone to, we had to stand ourselves.

Night 4 (The Train)

What were we doing on that train, as it rolled over and through and past everything in the huge darkness?

It was so open, our train. It was a roller coaster car with four shaky tin walls and a steel bar for ordering everything. We sat close, our arms carefully stacked, our hands in other hands. We arranged ourselves, turned our faces forward, touched our shoulders barely to each other. We sat straight and then forgot almost everything else.

The track rose and fell softly, thinly over a world of hill upon hill. There were no rivers or mountains or cities in our path, though we could see periodic flashes of distant light coming from over other hills as we sped past them through the cool darkness. The train just went and went, softly, silently, constantly on. And there was always your shoulder and the bar on my knees, and then only the night.

Nothing was in our way. What the train met, the train passed through. Everything in the world had two doors big enough. Every obstacle became a tunnel, every shape became an opening. There would be moments of change and then the sameness of night and shoulder again.

We passed calmly through a house-tunnel, caught a moment of dinner, a hand reaching for a bowl of beans, a father saying, "...her on the team if she..." and a boy squirming in a chair. We felt a moment around us and then there was a hill.

We passed serenely through a church-tunnel, found high walls and our necks craning to a ceiling of star and pillar, gold and dome, candle and echo. If the train never stopped, neither did it speed.

Hills and hills and always night like a bubble around us. Then we were there.

When the bar rose from our knees, we stepped out into an empty room. So the train passed us, kept sliding neatly on its way. We watched it become a train in the distance, stood in our empty room and held each other nervously. I wrapped my hair around us like a blanket. It had grown very long and I was proud.

Night 5 (The Bake Sale)

It was cold in my town, in the place where I live. Lucy and I were sad, walking beside each other in the cold, not speaking. I wanted her to cry, to finish with tears, but she wouldn't. The silence was buzzing, a fly trapped in a car. The silence of Lucy not speaking was something being torn too slowly, a piece of thick paper ripping for a year. Finally she walked away.

Alone, I looked at the sidewalk, counted the cracks and felt warm. "It's only that I'm walking fast," I told myself. But I took off my mittens and my hat, let them fall behind me. I shed my scarf the same way, walking faster. I slipped out of my coat as I felt one boot come unglued, stick in the mud, so I kicked at the other boot, let go.

I was down to my jeans and a little white blouse. My socks were gone and my feet were moving fast. My legs flashed like seconds and my hair shook itself loose and still I was warm, and I thought a flushed thought, thought a laugh and stopped. I stopped to swallow my thought and it was spring.

The trees were somehow green and wet and the sun was warm over the cool breeze and hot on the sidewalk. I was at an intersection, a familiar corner. I walked slowly east, noticing things, and when I came to a sign, I stopped. It said, "Bake Sale."

I was supposed to meet you! I was supposed to meet you at the Bake Sale. I was five minutes late, and so I ran inside and then a woman said in a hushed voice, "He's out back dear, through this door, into the garden you go."

I went into the garden.

There were peonies and morning glories, lilacs and daffodils. The garden was a bower and the bower was for sale, tables covered in icing, covered in blossoms. Sprinkled with sugar and sifted. You were there waiting.

I reached for a cake, grabbed for something to give you and what my fingers found was the smallest cake of all. It was the size of my hand, a little flat circle covered in hard sugar, filled with smaller circles, filled with even smaller circles than that. And inside each of the smallest circles were letters I could barely read. I looked close, looked hard. I stepped toward you with the little cake and you said, "Look again."

"I know. I know." I said. Each tiny circle held the smallest letters I had ever seen, written in the finest hand. As though etched, carved with an invisible pin, words again and again, over and over and over. They said, "I am happy I am happy I am happy."

In sugar.

Acknowledgments

Some of these poems first appeared elsewhere. Grateful acknowledgement is made.

"The Answer to the Puzzle", *Stickman Review*
"The Beast in the Cornfield", *Unpleasant Event Schedule*
"Elegy for the Fair", *Coconut*
"The Field Has a Girl", *Shampoo*
"The Girl Learns Forfeit", *Painted Bride Quarterly*
"Gravity of Halfway", *Unpleasant Event Schedule*
"Happily Ever After", *Post Road*
"In the Kitchen", *Parlorgames*
"Just There", *Coconut*
"Logos", *The Iowa Review*
"Night 1", *Double Room*
"Night 2", *The Styles*
"Night 3", *Double Room*
"Night 4", *Double Room*
"Night 5", *Double Room*
"Organizing the Stairs", *Stickman Review*
"Paper Dolls", *Drunken Boat*
"Posture Matters", *Blue Mesa Review*
"The Simple Machines", *Post Road*
"Technology", *BORN*
"Then Up—Shaken Morning", *Salt River Review*
"Triptych of Useful Rules", *Nidus*
"Weak Little Creatures", *Pip Lit*
"Well: the girl who falls", *Salt River Review*
"What the Dock Saw", *American Letters and Commentary*

About the Author

A Baltimore native, Laurel Snyder is a graduate of both the Iowa Writers' Workshop and the University of Tennessee at Chattanooga. She writes poems, essays, and children's books, and lives in Atlanta with her husband and two young sons. Her work (and life) can be found online at jewishyirishy.com.

Also by No Tell Books

2008

Personations, by Karl Parker

2007

The Bedside Guide to No Tell Motel - 2nd Floor, editors Reb Livingston & Molly Arden

Shy Green Fields, by Hugh Behm-Steinberg

Harlot, by Jill Alexander Essbaum

Never Cry Woof, by Shafer Hall

2006

The Bedside Guide to No Tell Motel, editors Reb Livingston & Molly Arden

Elapsing Speedway Organism, by Bruce Covey

The Attention Lesson, by PF Potvin

Navigate, Amelia Earhart's Letters Home, by Rebecca Loudon

Wanton Textiles, by Reb Livingston & Ravi Shankar

notellbooks.org

www.ingramcontent.com/pod-product-compliance
Lightning Source LLC
Chambersburg PA
CBHW031209090426
42736CB00009B/848